Experiments With Plants

CHRISTINE TAYLOR-BUTLER

Children's Press®
An Imprint of Scholastic Inc.
New York   Toronto   London   Auckland   Sydney
Mexico City   New Delhi   Hong Kong
Danbury, Connecticut

Content Consultant
Suzanne E. Willis, PhD
Professor and Assistant Chair, Department of Physics
Northern Illinois University
DeKalb, Illinois

Library of Congress Cataloging-in-Publication Data

Taylor-Butler, Christine.
  Experiments with plants/Christine Taylor-Butler.
     p. cm.—(A true book)
  Includes bibliographical references and index.
  ISBN-13: 978-0-531-26347-1 (lib. bdg.)   ISBN-13: 978-0-531-26647-2 (pbk.)
  ISBN-10: 0-531-26347-9 (lib. bdg.)   ISBN-10: 0-531-26647-8 (pbk.)
  1. Plants—Experiments—Juvenile literature. 2. Science
projects—Juvenile literature. I. Title.
  QK52.6.T393 2012
  580.78—dc22
                                                 2011010920

All rights reserved. Published in 2012 by Children's Press, an imprint of Scholastic Inc.
Printed in China 62
SCHOLASTIC, CHILDREN'S PRESS, A TRUE BOOK, and associated logos are trademarks and/or registered trademarks of Scholastic Inc.

1 2 3 4 5 6 7 8 9 10 R 21 20 19 18 17 16 15 14 13 12

Find the Truth!

Everything you are about to read is true *except* for one of the sentences on this page.

Which one is **TRUE**?

T or F Plants use all the water they take in from the ground.

T or F Some plants can eat rodents and lizards.

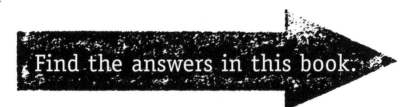

Find the answers in this book.

3

Contents

THE **BIG** TRUTH!

Anatomy of a Plant

**Apples growing
on a tree**

You can do the plant experiments in this True Book.

Sunflowers turn to face the sun.

Plants All Around Us

Look around you. The earth is filled with plants. There are more species of plants in the world than animals. Plants help clean the air. They produce the oxygen humans need to breathe. Their roots hold soil in place. They provide most of the food we eat. Some plants even provide the raw materials for the clothes we wear. Humans could not survive without plants.

The Amazon rainforest is so full of plant life, it is called the lungs of the world.

7

Sunflowers always point toward the sunlight.

The Lives of Plants

Plants start from tiny seeds or large bulbs. They wait for the right set of conditions to start growing. They can adapt to their conditions. For example, a cactus stores water so it can survive in the hot, dry desert. Sunflowers turn to follow the sun all day long until they are fully grown. Plants have adapted to many different growing conditions over millions of years.

Scientists who study plants are called botanists. They work in laboratories, outdoors, and in greenhouses to learn how plants live and grow. For example, they have learned that trees prepare for the winter by shutting down their food production. Scientists know that each part of a plant has a special function. They study why some plants grow once while others return every year.

Annual plants grow only one time. Perennials return each year.

Only two kinds of flowering plants are found in Antarctica.

9

The Scientific Method

You can learn about plants by using the scientific method. First, a scientist pulls together all the observations about something. Next, he or she thinks up a question that the observations don't explain. Then the scientist forms a **hypothesis**. This is what the scientist believes is the correct answer to the question. It must be a statement that can be tested. Next, he or she plans out an experiment to test it.

Botanists study plants to test their hypotheses.

About 25 percent of the medicine we use comes from plants.

You can learn a lot by experimenting with plants.

During the experiment, the scientist writes down everything that happens. Finally, the scientist looks at how the experiment turned out and draws a **conclusion**.

Sometimes, the conclusion is that the hypothesis is correct. Other times, it turns out that the hypothesis was not correct. Then it's time to come up with a new hypothesis and design another experiment.

Seeds: Tiny Life in a Package

Cut an apple in half. What do you see in the middle? Seeds that contain all the material needed to make a new plant. Seeds are dormant. That means they don't grow until the right conditions are present to help them start growing.

Apples, pears, plums, and peaches come from the same family of plants as roses.

Experiment #1: Knowing When to Grow

Observe: Most plants begin growing in the spring. Water falls and temperatures rise.

Research question: How much rain do seeds need?

True Book hypothesis: Seeds need a small amount of water to grow.

Materials:
- 12 dried lima beans
- water
- paper towels
- 3 sandwich bags
- ruler

Gather these materials.

Procedure:

1. Soak the dried lima beans in water overnight.

2. Place a damp paper towel in bag #1. Fill bag #2 halfway with water. Do not add water to bag #3.

3. Place 4 beans in each bag. Close the bags and set them in a sunny window.

4. Check the beans each day for one week.

5. Add water to the paper towel to keep it damp, but not soaking wet.

Step 4

Record your results: Which beans sprout first? How big are they? Do any beans not sprout?

Conclusion: Too much or too little water is bad for seeds. Seeds soaked in water will rot. Seeds without water won't be able to grow. Does this match your observations? Was the True Book hypothesis correct?

Experiment #2: Get the Dirt on It!

Observe: Plants grow in flower pots or in the ground outside.

Research question: Do plants grow out of a certain substance?

True Book hypothesis: Plants need soil to grow.

Seeds grow best with just the right amount of water.

Materials:

- **3 paper cups**
- **3 bean sprouts from the previous experiment (p. 13)**
- **potting soil**
- **sand**
- **pebbles**
- **water**
- **ruler**

Procedure:

1. Fill one cup with soil, one with sand, and one with pebbles.

2. Add water to each cup until the contents are moist.

3. Plant one bean sprout in each cup and place them in a sunny window.

4. Measure the height of the sprouts each day for one week.

Gather these materials.

16

Step 3

Record your results: Which sprout grows fastest? Are any sprouts not growing?

Conclusion: Seeds contain food for a new plant. When this food runs out, the plant needs nutrients from someplace else. Soil contains nutrients the plant can use. Pebbles and sand do not. Does this match your observations? Was the True Book hypothesis correct?

Anatomy of a Plant

Flowers produce seeds and attract insects to pollinate the plant.

Stems are the main support for the plant. Tubes inside the stem called xylem move water and nutrients throughout the plant.

Roots anchor the plant to the ground. They absorb water and nutrients from the ground.

Fruit protects seeds and helps them spread.

Seeds contain the material to make a new plant.

Leaves use sunlight and chlorophyll to turn carbon dioxide and water into food for the plant. This process is called photosynthesis.

Stomata are tiny holes in a plant's leaves. They allow water vapor to escape. Carbon dioxide enters each stoma. This helps with photosynthesis.

CHAPTER 3

Life Underground

When you look at a plant, you can see what happens above the ground. But what is happening below the ground? Roots are the foundation of a plant. They play an important role in its development. Roots burrow into the ground, and exchange water and nutrients with the earth. They also hold the plant firmly in place.

The roots of a California redwood tree can grow 900 feet (274 meters) long.

20

Experiment #1: How Long?

Observe: Roots have different lengths.

Research question: Are roots the same length as the rest of the plant?

True Book hypothesis: Roots are longer than stems.

Materials:

- 2 paper cups
- 2 saucers
- the 2 largest bean plants from the previous experiment (p. 16)

- potting soil
- water
- ruler

Choose your two largest bean plants.

Procedure:

1. Poke a hole in the bottom of each cup and place both on a saucer.

2. Fill the cups with potting soil and add water until moist.

3. Plant one bean sprout in each cup, keeping part of the shoot above the surface of the soil.

4. Set the cups in a sunny window.

5. Record your observations each day for one week.

6. After one week, take the plants out of their cups. Measure the height of the stems. Then measure the length of the roots.

How tall are your bean sprouts by the end of the experiment?

Record your results: Are the roots the same length as the plant on top?

Conclusion: The roots should be longer than the stems. Roots branch out and lengthen into the soil. This gives the plant stability. Does this match your observations? Was the True Book hypothesis correct?

Long roots anchor the plant in the ground.

Experiment #2: Taproots

Observe: All plants have roots.

Research question: What happens if part of a root is cut?

True Book hypothesis: A plant will be able to grow if part of its root is cut off.

Materials:
- raw carrot with greens
- knife
- small container, such as a drinking glass
- 1 cup of sand
- warm water

Be sure to ask an adult for help when using a sharp knife.

24

Procedure:

1. Ask an adult to help cut the carrot about 1 inch (3 centimeters) below the leaves. Cut off all the green leaves on top.

2. Fill the container with sand and sink the carrot top without leaves partway in the sand.

3. Pour water into the container to the top of the sand and place it in a sunny window.

4. Check on the carrot each day. Add water when the sand feels dry.

5. After four weeks, pull the carrot from the container.

Step 2

Record your results: Do new sprouts appear? How many days does it take? Are leaves growing? Do you grow a new carrot?

Conclusion: The carrot will grow new leaves. Most plants die when you cut their taproot, or main root. But carrots are different. Because carrots are root vegetables, they grow underground. The carrot top stores enough food and energy to make new leaves. Does this match your observations? Was the True Book hypothesis correct?

Carrots, beets, and turnips are all examples of root vegetables.

Corpse Flowers

The titan arum is the rarest flowering plant in the world. It grows in the rain forest of Indonesia. Titan arum is often called the corpse flower because it smells like rotting meat. It only blooms once every 1,000 days. The stalk grows up to 10 feet (3 m) tall and 3 feet (1 m) wide, and lasts for only three days. Titan arum grows from a type of fat root called a **tuber**.

Stems

Take a look at the trees outside. The trunk is the main stem of the tree. It provides support to keep the plant standing tall. If you cut straight through the trunk, you will see rings. The rings can tell you how old the tree is. But what else do stems do? How do the roots get water to the top of the trees?

It takes about 43 gallons (163 liters) of sap to make 1 gallon (4 l) of maple syrup.

28

Experiment #1: Capillary Action

Observe: Roots absorb water.

Research question: How does water travel through a plant?

True Book hypothesis: Water travels from the bottom of a plant to the top.

Materials:
- **tall glass**
- **water**
- **red food coloring**
- **2 stalks of celery**
- **spoon**
- **knife**
- **cutting board**
- **ruler**

Gather these materials.

Procedure:

1. Fill the glass halfway with water.

2. Add 10 drops of food coloring and stir well.

3. Cut 0.5 inch (1.3 cm) off the end of each celery stalk.

4. Place the stalks in the water.

5. Put the glass in a sunny window and let it sit for 12 hours.

6. Measure the height of the color in each stalk.

7. Cut 0.5 inch (1.3 cm) off the bottom of one stalk. What do you see?

8. Check the remaining celery stalk after 12 more hours.

Step 5

30

Record your results: How long does it take for the celery stalks to change color? What do you see on the bottom of the cut celery stalk?

Conclusion: The food coloring moves up the celery stalk through special tubes called xylem. As the food coloring shows, these tubes pull the water up. This pulling force is called **capillary** motion. Does this conclusion match your observations? Was the True Book hypothesis correct?

The red food coloring highlights the celery's xylem.

Ancient Greeks used celery for medicine instead of food.

Experiment #2: Osmosis!

Observe: Not all water is the same.

Research question: Can a plant survive in salt water?

True Book hypothesis: A plant cannot survive in salt water.

Materials:
- **2 tall glasses**
- **water**
- **a tablespoon**
- **salt**
- **a spoon**
- **masking tape**
- **2 stalks of fresh, crisp celery**

Gather these materials.

Procedure:

1. Fill both glasses halfway with water.

2. Stir 1 tablespoon (17 grams) of salt into one glass and mix well.

3. Use a piece of tape to label the glass "NaCl," which means salt.

4. Label the other glass "Plain H2O," for water.

5. Cut 1 inch (3 cm) from the bottom of each celery stalk.

6. Place one stalk in each glass and set them in a window. Let them sit overnight.

7. Take the celery stalks out of the water and try to bend them. Do they bend or break?

Step 6

8. Empty and pour fresh water into the glass marked "Plain H2o."

9. Cut 0.5 inch (1.3 cm) from the bottom of the limp celery stalk.

10. Place it into the glass and set it in a window. Let it sit overnight.

Record your results: In step 7, did either celery stalk bend? Did one break? Did they look the same? After step 10, was the celery limp or stiff?

Timeline of Plants on Earth

488–444 million years ago (MYA)
Plants begin to grow on land.

34

Conclusion: The stalk is made of tiny cells. Water can pass through the cell wall in a process called **osmosis**. If the glass of water contains more salt than the celery does, the water in the celery transfers into the glass. That is why the celery stalk in salt water became limp.

When the limp celery was placed in fresh water, it became stiff again. The celery contained more salt than the water, so the stalk took in water. Does this match your observations? Was the True Book hypothesis correct?

385–65.5 million years ago (MYA)
Plants with seeds begin to develop.

145–65.5 million years ago (MYA)
Some plants begin to grow flowers.

10 (MYA)
The Amazon Rainforest spreads across South America.

CHAPTER 5

Flowers and Leaves

Examine the leaves and petals of a flower. Are they the same on both sides? Why do leaves turn green in the summer and a different color in the winter? If stems help water travel through the plant, what do leaves and flowers do?

Experiment #1: Where Does the Water Go?

Observe: Xylem carry moisture through the plant.

Research question: What happens after the moisture reaches the leaves or flowers?

True Book hypothesis: A plant uses all of the water it takes in.

Materials:
- **tall glass**
- **water**
- **1 stem of pale flowers**
- **clear sandwich bag**
- **rubber band**

Gather all the materials you need.

Procedure:

1. Fill the glass halfway with water.

2. Cut 1 inch (3 cm) from the bottom of the flower stem and place the stem in the glass.

3. Cover the flower and some leaves with the sandwich bag.

4. Secure the bag with a rubber band, being sure not to squeeze all of the air out of the bag.

5. Put the flower in a sunny window and let it sit overnight.

Record your results: What do you see forming inside the plastic?

Conclusion: Moisture forms on the inside of the bag. This shows that plants don't use all of the water they take in. They put some of it into the air through tiny openings. Does this match your observations? Was the True Book hypothesis correct?

Step 4

A Venus flytrap traps more than flies.

Meat Eaters!

Some plants are carnivorous. They capture small prey and **secrete** special proteins to digest them. The Venus flytrap contains tiny hairs inside its leaves. The hairs act as a trigger. When an insect touches the hairs, the trap springs. In Borneo, pitcher plant leaves grow so large they can catch rodents, birds, and small lizards.

Experiment #2: It's Not Easy Being Green

Observe: Most plants are green.

Research question: Can the green color be removed from the plant?

True Book hypothesis: The green color can be removed from leaves.

Materials:
- scissors
- coffee filter
- coin
- dark green leaves
- rubbing alcohol
- small cup

You can try this experiment with leaves from more than one kind of plant.

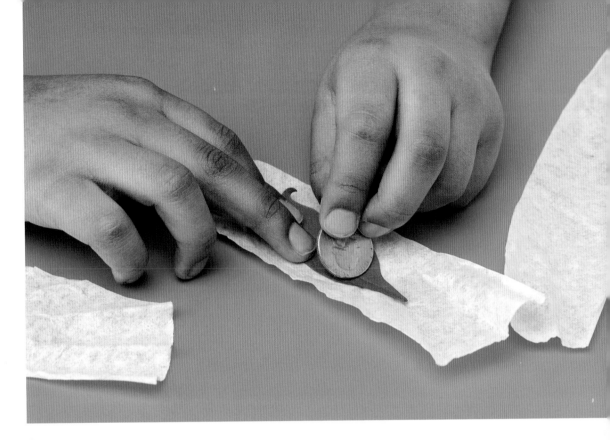

Step 2

Procedure:

1. Cut the coffee filter into strips.

2. Use the edge of a coin to rub a leaf against the strip. This leaves green marks on the filter.

3. Pour 0.5 inch (1.3 cm) of rubbing alcohol into the cup.

4. Dip the end of the coffee filter strip into the cup.

Record your results: What happens to the green color as the strip absorbs the liquid?

Conclusion: The green color can be removed from leaves. The filter strip turned yellow, orange, or red. Does this conclusion match your observations? Was the True Book hypothesis correct?

What happened? The rubbing alcohol in this experiment took away a **pigment** called chlorophyll. Chlorophyll makes plants green. In the fall, there is less sunlight and the chlorophyll goes away. The colors left behind show through. Fall leaves and our coffee filters showed the leaves' true colors. ★

Step 4

True Statistics

Number of plant species in the world: 350,000, and changing every day

Number of carnivorous plant species in the world: 600

Tallest tree in the world: Coast redwood, 385 ft. (117 m)

Tallest grass: Giant timber bamboo, which can grow 60 ft. (18 m) in two months

Largest flowering plant: Titan arum, or corpse flower, 170 lbs. (77 kg)

Largest leaf: Amazon water lily, 6 ft. (2 m) across

Smallest plant: Duckweed, 0.04 in. (0.1 cm)

Biggest seed: Coco de Mer, 66 lbs. (30 kg)

Did you find the truth?

(F) Plants use all the water they take in from the ground.

(T) Some plants can eat rodents and lizards.

Resources

Books

Aloian, Molly, and Bobbie Kalman. *The Life Cycle of a Flower*. New York: Crabtree Publishing, 2004.

Claybourne, Anna. *Growing Plants: Plant Life Processes*. Chicago: Heinemann Library, 2008.

Cook, Trevor. *Experiments With Plants and Other Living Things*. New York: PowerKids Press, 2009.

Gardner, Robert. *Ace Your Plant Science Project*. Berkeley Heights, NJ: Enslow Publishers, 2010.

Gray, Susan H. *Junior Scientists Experiments With Plants*. Ann Arbor, MI: Cherry Lake, 2010.

Riley, Peter D. *Plant Life*. New York: Franklin Watts, 2003.

Spohn, Rebecca. *Ready, Set, Grow! A Kid's Guide to Gardening*. Culver City, CA: Good Year Books 2007.

Organizations and Web Sites

Canopy in the Clouds—Tropical Montane Cloud Forest

www.canopyintheclouds.com

This interactive Web site has videos and facts about plants in this cloud forest in Costa Rica.

Missouri Botanical Garden—Biology of Plants

www.mbgnet.net/bioplants/main.html

Find facts about plants and a game to test your knowledge.

University of Illinois Extension—The Great Plant Escape

http://urbanext.illinois.edu/gpe/index.cfm

Solve mysteries involving plant life.

Places to Visit

Powell Gardens

1609 NW US Highway 50
Kingsville, MO 64061
(816) 697-2600
www.powellgardens.org
Visit the Heartland Harvest Garden exhibit to learn how foods make the journey from seeds to your plate.

United States Botanic Garden

100 Maryland Avenue SW
Washington, DC 20001
(202) 225-8333
www.usbg.gov
See many different kinds of plants and learn more about how they grow.

Important Words

capillary (KAP-uh-ler-ee)—tiny vessel that is one cell thick

chlorophyll (KLOR-uh-fil)—the green substance in plants that uses sunlight to make food from carbon dioxide and water

conclusion (kuhn-KLOO-zhun)—final decision

hypothesis (hy-PAH-thuh-siss)—a prediction that can be tested about how a scientific experiment or investigation will turn out

osmosis (ahs-MOH-sis)—the process in which a more concentrated solution moves through a cell membrane to a less concentrated solution

photosynthesis (foh-toh-SIN-thi-sis)—the process in which plants use energy from the sun to make food

pigment (PIG-muhnt)—a substance that gives color to something

secrete (si-KREET)—to produce and release a liquid

stomata (STOH-mah-tuh)— the plural of stoma, the opening in a plant wall that lets water and air pass through

tuber (TOO-bur)—thick underground stem of a plant, such as a potato

xylem (ZYE-luhm)—tubes in plant stems that carry water from the roots to the rest of the plant

Index

Page numbers in **bold** indicate illustrations

About the Author

Christine Taylor-Butler is the award-winning author of more than sixty books for children including a True Book series on American Government as well as another on Health and the Human Body. A graduate of the Massachusetts Institute of Technology (MIT), she is passionate about finding fun ways to introduce science, technology, engineering and math (STEM) concepts to children. Christine lives in Kansas City, Missouri.

10